# SELENA GOMEZ

By Maria Nelson

Gareth Stevens
Publishing

**Please visit our website, www.garethstevens.com. For a free color catalog of all our high-quality books, call toll free 1-800-542-2595 or fax 1-877-542-2596.**

Nelson, Maria.
 Selena Gomez / Maria Nelson.
     p. cm. — (Rising stars)
 Includes bibliographical references and index.
 ISBN 978-1-4339-5904-2 (pbk.)
 ISBN 978-1-4339-5905-9 (6-pack)
 ISBN 978-1-4339-5902-8 (library binding)
 1. Gomez, Selena, 1992—Juvenile literature. 2. Actors—United States—Biography—Juvenile literature. 3. Singers—United States—Biography—Juvenile literature. I. Title.
 PN2287.G585N45 2011
 791.4302'8092—dc22
 [B]

                            2010046768

First Edition

Published in 2012 by
**Gareth Stevens Publishing**
111 East 14th Street, Suite 349
New York, NY 10003

Designer: Katelyn E. Reynolds
Editor: Kristen Rajczak

Photo credits: Cover, pp. 1–32 (background) Shutterstock.com; cover, p. 1 Jason Merritt/Getty Images; pp. 5, 21 Shutterstock.com; p. 7 Michael Tran/FilmMagic; p. 9 Frederick M. Brown/Getty Images; p. 11 K Mazur/TCA 2008/WireImage; p. 13 John M. Heller/Getty Images; p. 15 Kevin Winter/Getty Images for KCA; p. 17 George Pimentel/WireImage; p. 19 Stephen Lovekin/Getty Images; p. 23 Kevin Winter/DCNYRE2010/Getty Images for DCP; p. 25 Paul Hiffmeyer/Disney via Getty Images; p. 27 Alberto E. Rodriguez/Getty Images; p. 29 Joe Corrigan/Getty Images.

Printed in the United States of America

CPSIA compliance information: Batch #CS11GS: For further information contact Gareth Stevens, New York, New York at 1-800-542-2595.

# Contents

# Meet Selena

Selena Gomez is an actress and singer.

She is named after the famous

Mexican American singer Selena.

Selena is from Grand Prairie, Texas. She was born July 22, 1992. Selena and her mom now live in the city of Los Angeles, California.

Selena's mom, Mandy Cornett

# Starting Small

Selena started acting when she was 7 years old! Her first acting job was on the TV show *Barney & Friends*. She was on the show for 2 years.

# Disney Darling

Selena was first on the Disney Channel in 2006. She was on *The Suite Life of Zack and Cody.* In 2007 and 2008, Selena played Mikayla on *Hannah Montana.*

Miley Cyrus

In 2007, Selena started playing Alex Russo in the *Wizards of Waverly Place*. Alex is a witch. Selena also sings the TV show's theme song.

David Henrie

Maria Canals-Barrera

Jennifer Stone

Jake T. Austin

13

Selena won a 2010 Teen Choice Award for the *Wizards of Waverly Place*. She also won a Nickelodeon Kids' Choice Award!

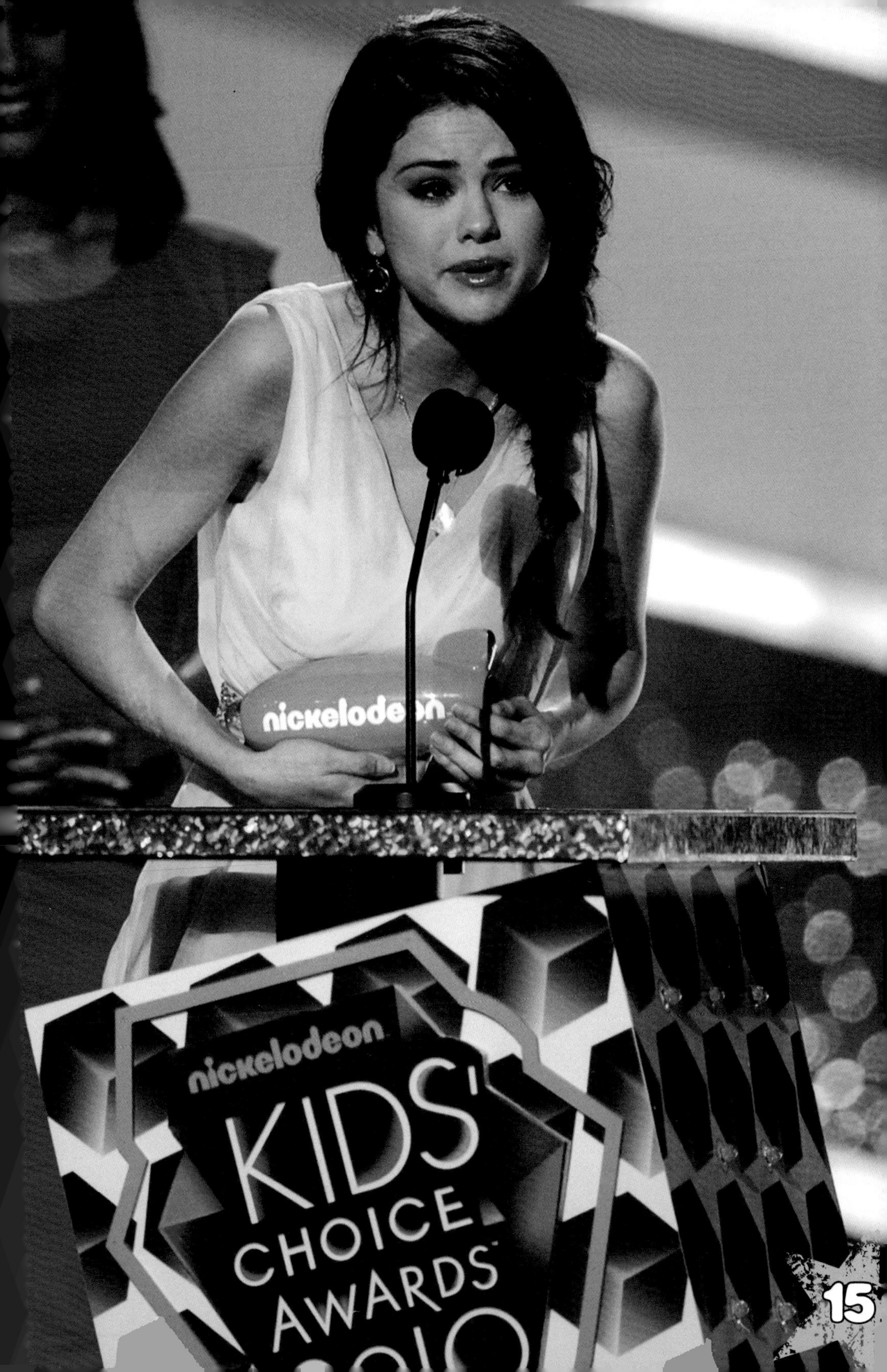
nickelodeon
nickelodeon
KIDS'
CHOICE
AWARDS

Selena played Carter in the Disney Channel movie *Princess Protection Program* in 2009. Her friend Demi Lovato was in the movie, too. Demi and Selena met on *Barney & Friends*.

Demi Lovato

# On the Big Screen

In 2010, Selena was in the movie *Ramona and Beezus*. She played Beezus Quimby. Selena was in the movie *Monte Carlo* in 2011.

Joey King

# The Music Scene

Selena and her band put out the album *Kiss & Tell* in September 2009. The band is called Selena Gomez and the Scene. Their song "Naturally" made Billboard's Hot 100 list.

In 2009, Selena and the band were on TV on New Year's Eve. She sang "Naturally." Selena shared the stage with Justin Bieber.

Justin Bieber

Selena Gomez and the Scene put out *A Year Without Rain* in September 2010. The album made the Billboard Top 200. The song "A Year Without Rain" made the Hot 100.

# Trendsetter

Selena has a clothing line. It's called
Dream Out Loud by Selena Gomez.
She has won two Teen Choice Awards
for how well she dresses.

# Doing Good

Selena is an ambassador for the
United Nations Children's Fund.
She raises money to help children
all over the world.

# Timeline

**1992**    Selena is born on July 22.

**2007**    Selena is on *Hannah Montana*. *Wizards of Waverly Place* starts.

**2009**    Selena stars in *Princess Protection Program*.
The album *Kiss & Tell* comes out.

**2010**    Selena stars in *Ramona and Beezus*.
The album *A Year Without Rain* comes out.

**2011**    The movie *Monte Carlo* comes out.

# For More Information

## Books

Harte, Harlee. *I (heart) Selena Gomez*. Beverly Hills, CA: Dove Books, 2009.

Rutherford, Lucy. *Demi Lovato & Selena Gomez: The Complete Unofficial Story of the BFFs*. Toronto, ON, Canada: ECW Press, 2009.

## Websites

**Selena Gomez**

*www.imdb.com/name/nm1411125/*

Find out more about Selena Gomez's movies and TV shows.

**Selena Gomez's Official Website**

*selenagomez.com*

Keep up with the latest news about Selena Gomez.

# Glossary

**ambassador:** a person who acts for a group

**award:** a prize given for doing something well

**theme song:** a song that begins a TV show

# Index